MW00710725

ATR Publishing

Amy's Favorite Recipes

by Amy Lawrence

Published by:
ATR Publishing

Cover Photo by:
Airic van Staveren
http://www.airic.com/

Back Cover Photo by:
Sirlin Photographers
(916)444-8464
http://www.sirlin.com/

On the cover:
Four Layer German Chocolate Cake (top-left, page 141)
Choc Bars (top-right, page 133)
Fruit Pizza (bottom-right, page 147)
Reuben Egg Rolls (bottom-left, page 31)

Foreword

I'm dedicating this cookbook to all of the loyal tea room customers of An Afternoon to Remember. You are the reason I ever decided to start writing cookbooks. The first year the tea room was opened, you began requesting our recipes. Those requests prompted me to write my first cookbook in 2004. From that moment on, I wrote a cookbook every year with the year's best recipes. In all, I have now written a total of 8 cookbooks, including the Scone Book Collection and the Master Tea Room Recipes. I've sold over 10,000 of them, thanks to you!

I would also like to thank my family for their love and support. They've really had fun with this cookbook as I've written it all from home, testing out each recipe again on them. Of course, no one deserves more thanks than my husband. He's the reason the books ever get printed. Without his expertise, I would be lost. Actually without him, I would be lost as well – he's the love of my life.

Out of all of the cookbooks I've written, this one has been the most fun of all. Maybe it's because each recipe reminds me of home, family and friends. Most of the recipes I remember where I lived when I first had the dish, received the recipe or created the dish. In a way, it's like a diary of my military brat life. I've moved 18 times in my life, lived in 7 different states and in four different cities in Germany.

The recipes are as I make them. Of course you can always

Foreword Continued

lighten things up a bit by using less butter, light sour cream, cream cheese or mayonnaise but I'm giving you the best way to make them. My motto is moderation. Personally I'd rather have a little of the dish versus using fat-free or reduced ingredients. However, everyone is different and has different dietary preferences. Obviously I don't cook rich-laden dishes every day, but these are my special ones.

I'm always amazed how impressed people are when I make these dishes. Really the recipes aren't hard to make at all. We live in such a hectic world these days that many people do not really take the time to cook anymore. Most of these dishes do not take much time. So don't be scared if it says, "Homemade Pudding." Once you make it, you will never go back to instant again. It's that good and probably much better for you. So be good to yourself and take a bit of time to make something extraordinary. You'll be glad you did!

Happy cooking!

With much love,

Amy

Table of Contents

Appetizers

Main Dishes

Table of Contents Continued

Main Dishes

Desserts

Table of Contents Continued

Desserts

Drinks

Appetizers

Afternoon to Remember's Famous Pea Salad

This makes a big bowl! If you need to stretch it out a bit to serve more, add more peas. This is a very rich salad so you don't need to serve a huge portion to your guests.

- 1 pkg. frozen peas
- ½ c. cashews, chopped – save a few tablespoons out for garnishing top of salad
- 1 c. celery, finely chopped
- 6 bacon strips, cooked crumbled – save a few tablespoons out for garnish
- ½ c. feta cheese – save a few tablespoons out for garnish
- ¼ c. red onion, chopped
- ½ c. mayo
- 1 pkg. Good Seasons Italian Salad Dressing Mix
- black pepper

In a large salad bowl, mix together peas, cashews, celery, bacon, red onion and feta. In a small bowl, mix together mayo and salad dressing mix. Add salad dressing mix to pea mixture. Mix well. If you need more mayonnaise to hold it together, add a bit more. (I don't like mine with so much mayo.) Garnish top with a few tablespoons of cashews, bacon and feta. Sprinkle with black pepper.

Notes

Baked Brie Appetizer

This is a very easy and elegant appetizer.

- 1 round block of brie
- 1 sheet of frozen puff pastry
- ½ of an onion, chopped
- 1 T. butter
- ½-¾ c. dried cranberries or Craisins
- 1 egg white, beaten

Preheat oven to 400°. Thaw out frozen puff pastry sheet for about 30 minutes. Do not thaw too long as it will stick together. In a skillet, brown onions in the butter until they caramelize. Allow to cool.

Scrape all of the white rind off of the brie with a knife. Carefully top brie with the grilled onions. Top with the cranberries/Craisins. nwrap puff pastry. Trim off corners and save. Stretch pastry over the top of the cranberries and brie. Carefully tuck ends underneath the brie. Roll out the saved corners and cut into leaf shapes. Place the leaf shapes on top of the brie.

Brush pastry-covered brie with egg white and bake until golden brown (for about 20 minutes). Allow to sit at room temperature for about 40 minutes.

Serve with crackers.

Notes

Black Bean Dip

I love this dip and it's very healthy, unless you overdo it on the tortilla chips or cheese.

- 3 15 oz. cans of black beans, drained
- 2 t. vegetable oil
- 1 c. chopped onion
- 4 garlic cloves, minced
- 1 c. diced tomato
- ⅔ c. salsa (can be mild, medium or hot depending on how you like it)
- 1½ t. ground cumin
- 1½ t. chili powder
- ¾ c. shredded Monterey Jack cheese (can use reduced fat if you prefer)
- ½ c. chopped fresh cilantro
- 3 T. lime juice

Heat oil in a medium non-stick skillet. Add onion and garlic and sauté until tender. Add beans, tomato, salsa, cumin and chili powder. Cook about 5 minutes or until thickened slightly. Turn off heat. Add remaining ingredients.

Serve warm or at room temperature with tortilla chips.

Note: Before adding the beans, you can partially mash them, I like them whole, but the original recipe called for partly mashed.

Notes

Broccoli Salad

This is a classic and tastes great the next day. My husband loves to make it. Aren't I lucky?

- 3-4 bunches of broccoli, chopped
- 1 red onion, chopped
- ¾ c. raisins, red currants or Craisins
- ½ c. sunflower seeds, hulled
- ½ lb. bacon, cooked crisp and cut into tiny pieces

Dressing:

- ¾ c. mayonnaise
- 2-3 T. apple cider vinegar
- 3-4 T. sugar

In a large bowl, mix together salad ingredients. In a small bowl or measuring cup, mix together dressing ingredients. Pour dressing over salad and toss. Add sunflower seeds and bacon at serving time.

Serves 4-6.

Notes

Cauliflower Salad

I grew up on this salad. Unfortunately I don't make it too often as my family doesn't like cauliflower, but it's so delicious. My mother makes a lighter version by using light mayonnaise and 5 packets of Splenda instead of sugar.

- 1 head cauliflower
- 1 head iceberg lettuce or green lettuce
- 1 medium onion, chopped
- 1 pound bacon, fried and crumbled
- 1 c. shredded sharp cheddar or grated Parmesan cheese
- salt and pepper, to taste

Dressing:
- 2 c. mayonnaise
- 1 T. sugar

In a very large mixing bowl, mix chopped cauliflower, lettuce, onion, bacon, cheese, salt and pepper. Pour dressing over the top and serve.

Notes

Cream Cheese Pizza Dip

This is very easy and takes no time at all to make if you have all of the ingredients on hand. You can add more ingredients or use less as desired.

- 1 8 oz. pkg. cream cheese, softened
- 1 jar of Heinz chili sauce
- 1 green/red pepper, chopped
- ½ c. onion, chopped
- ½ c. fresh mushrooms, sliced, or canned
- 1 tomato, chopped
- 1 t. oregano, optional
- 1 c. cheese (I like to use mozzarella and cheddar mixed, but any kind will do)

Spread softened cream cheese in a pie plate (on the sides and bottom). Add jar of chili sauce. Decorate like a pizza with the remaining ingredients.

Serve with crackers.

Notes

Fertita's Mexican Cheese Roll

I attended a New Year's party one year with my parents. The hostess made this, I loved it so much I came home and recreated the recipe.

- 1 lb. Velveeta Cheese loaf
- 1 8 oz. pkg. cream cheese, softened
- 1 small jar pimentos, well-drained
- 4 slices of bacon, cooked, finely chopped
- 1 small can black olives, well-drained, finely chopped
- ¼ c. green olives, well-drained, finely chopped
- 1 jalapeño, finely chopped
- 4 green onions, finely chopped
- ¼ c. fresh parsley, finely chopped, optional
- paprika

Between parchment paper or waxed paper, roll out Velveeta cheese with a rolling pin into a large rectangle about ¼ inch thick. Spread cream cheese over Velveeta. Sprinkle pimentos, bacon, olives, jalapeño, parsley over cream cheese. Fold Velveeta carefully in half. Sprinkle with paprika. Place on a platter. Before serving, microwave for just a bit to melt the cheese.

Serve with crackers.

Notes

Ginny's Chipped Beef Dip

When I was in the 6th grade, we lived in Naperville, Illinois, right next door to my best friend Diana. Her mother was an outstanding cook. They always had great parties at their house. I loved to watch her cook. She knew how fascinated I was and always took the time to explain what she was doing. I remember being in awe when she made Beef Wellington. Too bad she didn't give me that recipe! But she did give me this one. It's delicious, very easy and makes a great cracker spread.

- 1 8 oz. pkg. cream cheese
- 1 lg. pkg. chipped beef or corned beef, chopped
- 4-6 green onions, chopped
- milk

In a small bowl, combine all ingredients. Add enough milk to desired consistency. Use dip to spread on crackers.

Notes

Granny's Apples

My grandmother made these every holiday and my mom continues the tradition, as do I. My grandmother liked to add red hot cinnamon candies, which would turn the apples red. They were perfect for Christmas time.

- 1 c. sugar
- 1 c. water
- 1 quart peeled apples, cored and cut into quarters
- 1 lemon sliced
- 2 t. cinnamon

Combine sugar and water and bring to a boil. Add apples. Cover and cook slowly until syrup boils. Continue cooking gently pressing the apples down occasionally with a spoon until they are tender and translucent looking (about 20-30 minutes). If you cook them too long, they'll be too fragile and you'll have applesauce. So cook them just until translucent. Turn off heat. Add cinnamon and slices of lemon.

Serve in the syrup, hot or cold. (I think they are the best cold the next day!)

Notes

Keri's Guacamole

I used to teach for Placer County as a special education teacher. This recipe came from one of our assistants. It's the best guacamole ever! I receive compliments on it every time I bring it to a party.

- 2 avocados, ripe
- ¼ of a white onion, finely chopped
- 3 cloves garlic
- ½ jalapeño or to taste, chopped finely, optional
- 1 tomato, chopped
- 2 t. sherry or more to taste
- salt and pepper to taste

Cut each avocado in half. Pull out pit and place in serving bowl (this helps to prevent the guacamole from browning). Mash avocado into bowl. Add remaining ingredients.

Serve with tortilla chips.

Notes

Reuben Egg Rolls

I first had these at my favorite restaurant "Forge in the Forest," in Carmel, California. This is my rendition of them. Be sure and serve them with Thousand Island Dressing.

- 1 pkg. large square wrappers (egg roll wrappers)
- 1 lb. cooked corned beef (from the deli), sliced
- 2 c. cabbage, finely chopped
- 2 c. swiss cheese, shredded
- 1 egg, beaten
- vegetable oil
- 1 bottle of Thousand Island dressing for dipping sauce

Chop corned beef into small pieces. Finely chop cabbage. In a medium mixing bowl combine together: corned beef, cabbage, swiss cheese, salt and pepper to taste.

Beat egg in a small bowl. Take egg roll wrappers out of package and place on a large cutting board. Place a damp paper towel over wrappers while you work.

Place a wrapper on the cutting board, with a point side toward you. Spoon about ⅛-¼ c. of meat mixture into the center of the wrapper. Dip finger into egg and spread it onto opposite triangle of wrapper. Roll up egg roll about half-way and pull in edges, continue rolling and seal outside of point with more beaten egg. Place on a cookie sheet lined with parchment paper. Place a damp paper towel over the top so the egg rolls do not dry out. Refrigerate until you are ready to fry them (do not leave in refrigerator more than 1 day). Although I

Notes

Reuben Egg Rolls Continued

think they taste best the same day, you can also freeze them. Flash freeze them on the cookie sheet and then transfer to a ziplock bag. When you're ready to use them, thaw them out slightly before frying them.

To fry:

Heat deep fryer or oil in a pan on stove to about 375°. Deep fry until golden brown. Drain on paper towels and serve with a side dish of Thousand Island dressing.

Makes about 20 egg rolls (I like to cut them in half before serving them which would give you about 40 egg rolls).

Notes

Rhenee's Texas Caviar

This recipe came from a friend in Breckenridge, Colorado. We vacationed there at my aunt's time share. Rhenee and her husband invited over for dinner and served this with tortilla chips. It's delicious and serves a crowd!

- 1 lb. dried black eyed peas (sometimes I use canned to save time)
- 1-2 c. Italian salad dressing, (if you are using canned black eyed peas, 1 c. of dressing is fine because there is so much moisture in the peas)
- 2 c. red pepper, chopped or mixed peppers (red, yellow, orange)
- 1 ½ c. onion, chopped finely
- ½ c. green pepper, chopped finely
- 1 (3 oz) jar pimento, drained
- 1 T. garlic, minced or more if you like garlic
- 1 t. salt or to taste
- Tabasco to taste (I like to use quite a bit of Tabasco – 1 T. as I like it spicy.)

Soak peas 6 hours or overnight. Drain well. Place in saucepan. Cover with water. Bring to boil over high heat. Reduce heat. Simmer until tender (45 minutes or so). Drain and cool. Add remaining ingredients. Refrigerate.

Serve with corn chips or tortilla chips.

Notes

Roasted Garlic Herb Dip

I have used this recipe also to make cucumber tea sandwiches.
Just spread dip on bread which has been cut into rounds and
decorate with a cucumber.

- 8 cloves garlic
- 2 T. fresh basil, chopped
- 1 T. fresh thyme
- ⅔ c. cream cheese, softened
- ¼ c. mayonnaise
- 2 T. fresh chives, chopped
- ⅛ t. salt
- ⅛ t. pepper

Preheat oven to 500°. Wrap garlic cloves in foil and bake for
30 minutes. Squeeze cloves to extract pulp; discard skins. In
a food processor, mix garlic pulp, basil, thyme, cream cheese,
mayonnaise, chives, salt and pepper. Process until very
smooth. Spoon mixture into a bowl and chill.

Serve with vegetables, crackers, bagel chips or spread on
French bread.

Makes about 1 cup.

Notes

Sausage and Herb Stuffed Mushrooms

You can make these ahead of time and bake them right before your guests arrive.

- 20 medium-sized mushrooms
- ½ lb. pork sausage, can be hot if desired (I use Jimmy Dean)
- 3 cloves garlic, minced
- 2 green onions, finely chopped
- 6 T. total of chopped fresh herbs such as tarragon, chervil, basil, chives, thyme, rosemary, etc.
- 2 T. dry white wine
- salt and pepper
- 2 T. melted butter

Cook sausage in skillet until almost done. Drain well. Remove stems from mushrooms and chop stems finely. Melt 1 T. butter in a small skillet and sauté stems and green onion until soft. Add garlic, chopped herbs and wine. Season with salt and pepper. Add cooked sausage. Fill mushroom caps with filling and set in a greased baking dish. Brush with a little melted butter and bake at 375° for 7-10 minutes or until golden brown. Serve immediately.

Makes about 20 appetizers.

Notes

Sausage Balls

These are the perfect appetizers. They can be made ahead and frozen until ready to use. Just thaw slightly and bake immediately before guests arrive. They are perfect for breakfast and brunch as well!

- 1 lb. pork sausage (I use Jimmy Dean, hot style)
- 1½ lb. ground beef
- 1 t. Worcestershire Sauce
- 2 t. pepper
- 2 cloves garlic, minced
- 1 onion, finely chopped
- 3 c. baking mix, such as Bisquick
- 3 c. Monterey Jack cheese, shredded

Preheat oven to 375°. Mix all ingredients together. Roll into 1 inch balls. Place on a cookie sheet and bake for about 15 minutes or until meat is done. Serve hot.

Makes a lot!

Notes

Vegetable Pizza Appetizer

My first teaching job was in Topeka, Kansas at an inner-city elementary school. This recipe came from one of my co-workers who was also a teacher.

- 2 pkg. Crescent roll dough
- 1 egg white
- 1 pkg. Hidden Valley Ranch dressing mix
- 8 oz. cream cheese
- 1 c. mayonnaise
- ½ c. sour cream
- 1½ c. finely grated cheese (cheddar, jack, etc.)
- 5 c. finely chopped vegetables – broccoli, cauliflower, carrots, peppers, green onion, mushrooms, red cabbage, etc.

Preheat oven to 350°. Lightly spray an 11"x17" jelly roll pan with non-stick spray. Lightly unroll crescent roll dough flat in pan. Pinch all seams together. Use egg white as "glue" if necessary. Brush remaining egg white over dough and bake for 10-12 minutes or until lightly browned. Cool.

Meanwhile, beat dressing mix, cream cheese, mayo and sour cream until smooth. Chop selected vegetables as small as possible. A food processor works well on broccoli, carrots, and cheese, but destroys peppers and mushrooms. Cover baked dough with cream cheese mixture and spread vegetables over area evenly. Press into spread. Cover with cheeses. Press into spread.

Can be served right away, but it's best when made the night before. Cut into squares before serving.

Notes

Main Dishes

Amy's Chicken Tacos

I watched my neighbor Kelly fry the tortillas one day and my tacos have never been the same since. If I don't have the seasoning mix, then I just sprinkle oregano, cumin, chili pepper, and a little cayenne pepper over the chicken.

- 4 boneless, skinless chicken breasts
- 1 pkg. taco seasoning mix (chicken taco seasoning, if you can find it)
- flour tortillas
- parmesan cheese
- salt
- vegetable oil
- 2 cloves garlic, minced

Taco toppings: use some, all or more if desired!

- cheddar cheese, shredded
- fresh cilantro, chopped
- onions, chopped finely
- jalapeño, chopped finely
- black olives, chopped
- tomatoes, chopped
- salsa
- sour cream

Cut chicken into bite-sized pieces. Place 1 T. vegetable oil or olive oil in a large skillet. Add chicken and minced garlic. Pour ½ c. water in a liquid measuring cup. Add spice packet.

Notes

Amy's Chicken Tacos Continued

Stir well. Pour over chicken. Cook until chicken is done.

To make taco shells:

Place enough oil in a skillet to cover tortilla. Heat until hot. Carefully place tortilla in oil. Fry for a minute or so until browned, breaking air bubbles with fork. Turn tortilla over and fry until golden brown. Remove to a plate covered with paper towels. Drain slightly, then sprinkle parmesan cheese and salt over one side of tortilla. Fold in half and place in a taco holder or baking dish. Continue frying tortillas until you have the number you need. When finished, add chicken and toppings to fried tortilla and serve.

Notes

Asian Greens

I was introduced to kale and swiss chard from my veggie man, Jim Muck. I can't get enough of them! Some people like them on the softer side, if so, then add a cover to the skillet and cook a bit longer on low.

- 1 large bunch of Dinosaur Kale or Swiss Chard or combo
- 1 T. sesame oil
- ¼ c. chopped onions
- 2 cloves garlic, minced
- 1 t. grated ginger root
- 3 T. low-sodium soy sauce
- 2 T. toasted sesame seeds

Wash kale/swiss chard well. Fold the kale/swiss chard in half, cut along the stem and discard the tough rib, then chop coarsely into pieces. Set aside. In a large skillet or wok, heat the sesame oil over medium heat. Add the garlic and onions. Fry for a few minutes. Add the kale/swiss chard and cook for about 4-5 minutes until the leaves have softened but are not wilted. Add soy sauce, sesame seeds and ginger. Cook for another minute.

Serves about 2-3.

Notes

Baked Chicken and Black Bean Chimichangas

My kids love this recipe and it's very healthy if you omit the cheese and don't overdo it on the guacamole and sour cream.

- 4 boneless, skinless chicken breasts
- 2 cloves of garlic, minced
- 2 t. olive oil
- ¾ c. onion, finely chopped
- 2 t. cumin
- 1 t. pepper
- ½-¾ c. salsa (mild or hot)
- 1 small can green chilies
- 1-2 cans black beans, drained
- ½ c. shredded cheddar cheese, optional
- 1 pkg. flour tortillas

Toppings: Use as many as desired

- salsa
- sour cream
- chopped tomatoes
- guacamole
- chopped jalapeños
- black olives

Preheat oven to 425°. Heat oil in a non-stick skillet. Add garlic and onion. Sauté until tender. Chop chicken into small bite-sized pieces. Add to skillet. Add cumin and

Notes

Baked Chicken and Black Bean Chimichangas
Continued

pepper. Cook until chicken is almost done. Stir in salsa, green chilies and black beans. Cook until thoroughly heated.

Spray a 9"x13" baking dish with non-stick cooking spray. Warm tortilla slightly to prevent cracking and breaking when you roll it. Place about ¼ c. of chicken filling on a tortilla. Sprinkle cheese on top if desired. Fold in ends and roll up. Secure ends with tooth picks. Place in baking dish. Continue filling tortillas until filling is gone. Brush chimichangas with a small bit of olive oil (or spray with cooking spray). Bake for 20 minutes.

Makes about 14 small chimichangas if you use 7 inch tortillas.

Serve with toppings, rice or refried beans.

Notes

Baked Potato Soup

This was always too rich to serve at the tea room, but it's perfect for a main meal on a cold and rainy day.

- 4 large baking potatoes
- ⅔ c. butter
- ⅔ c. flour
- 6 c. of milk
- ¾ t. salt
- ½ t. pepper
- 4 green onions, chopped and divided
- 2 garlic cloves, minced
- 12 slices of bacon, cooked, crumbled and divided
- 1¼ c. cheddar cheese, shredded
- 8 oz. sour cream

Bake potatoes at 400° for one hour; let cool. Cut in half length-wise, and scoop out pulp. Set aside. Discard skins.

Melt butter in a heavy sauce pan over low heat. Add flour. Stir until smooth. Cook one minute, stirring constantly. Gradually add milk. Cook over medium heat, stirring constantly until mixture is thickened and bubbly.

Add potato pulp, salt, pepper, 2 T. green onion, 2 minced garlic cloves, ½ c. crumbled bacon and 1 c. cheese. Cook until thoroughly heated, then stir in sour cream. Add extra milk, if necessary.

Serve with remaining green onions, bacon and cheese. Makes about 10 cups. It's even better if reheated the next day.

Notes

Beef Stroganoff

This is one of my favorite main dishes. It takes me a little extra time to make it because I make 2 separate batches, one with mushrooms, one without – as my family does not like mushrooms. The original recipe called for Reams frozen egg noodles, but I can never find them in California. So I use my homemade egg noodle recipe found in this book (page 73), or if I'm in a hurry, I'll use store-bought dried egg noodles, but they definitely are not as good as the homemade ones. This recipe makes great left-overs. You can even serve them on toast.

- 1½ lbs. round steak
- flour
- salt and pepper
- ¼ c. butter
- ½-1 c. mushrooms, I like fresh, but you can use canned
- ½ c. onion, chopped
- 2 cloves of garlic, minced
- 1 can beef broth
- 1 can cream of chicken soup
- 1 c. sour cream
- ¼ c. flour

Cut steak into thin strips. Place in a plastic bag with a little flour, salt and pepper. Shake until well coated. Brown meat in butter. Add mushrooms, onion, garlic and brown lightly. Stir in beef broth. Cover and cook one hour. Add soup, cook 30 more minutes. Gradually stir in sour cream.

Serve over noodles.

Makes about 6 servings.

Notes

Caribbean Black Bean Soup

This recipe came from my mother's Army wife group when they were stationed in Texas. It's perfect on a winter day!

- 1 lb. black beans, or use canned black beans
- Water
- 4 slices bacon
- 3 large onions, chopped
- 4 cloves garlic, minced
- 1 red or green pepper, chopped
- 1 c. celery
- 2 cans tomatoes
- 2 t. cumin
- ½ t. thyme
- 1 lg. bay leaf
- 1 t. oregano
- ½ t. basil
- 2 c. smoked ham, chopped
- ½ c. dry sherry
- 3 T. red wine vinegar
- 2 small jars of pimentos, chopped
- 1 can green chiles
- Tabasco, to taste (I like it hot!)
- salt and pepper, to taste

Cover beans with cold water and soak for at least 5 hours (or

Notes

Caribbean Black Bean Soup Continued

overnight). Fry bacon in a large soup pot until browned. Crumble and set aside. To the drippings in the pot, add onions, garlic, red/green pepper and celery. Sauté until soft. Add tomatoes and simmer for a few minutes. Add spices. Add black beans and the liquid from the beans. Add ham. Bring to a boil, reduce heat and simmer for about 3 hours. When beans are tender, stir in sherry, vinegar, Tabasco, pimentos, salt and pepper. Cook another 30 minutes. Add crumbled bacon and serve with a dollop of sour cream and fresh chopped cilantro.

Makes about 8 servings.

Notes

Chicken Divan

My son Jacob liked to call this Chicken in a Van when he was younger. My mother made this often when I was growing up. I've made a few changes over the years.

- 4 boneless, skinless chicken breasts, cut up into bite-sized pieces
- 2 c. broccoli, cooked
- 2 cans cream of chicken soup
- ½ c. white wine, optional
- 1 c. mayonnaise
- 1 c. sour cream
- 1 T. lemon juice
- 1-2 t. curry
- ½ c. onion, finely chopped
- 2 c. sharp cheddar cheese
- 2 c. bread cubes (use slices of any bread and chop into small squares)
- butter

Preheat oven to 350°. Place chicken in a pan, cover with water and cook on stove for about 20 minutes until done. Drain and chop into bite-sized pieces. Cook broccoli in microwave or over stove in boiling water until just tender. (I often use cook the broccoli in the hot water from the chicken.) Drain and chop into bite-sized pieces.

In a medium bowl mix together: soup, mayonnaise,

Notes

Chicken Divan Continued

lemon juice, curry, wine, finely chopped onions. Spray a 9"x13" casserole dish with non-stick cooking spray. Layer cooked broccoli and chicken. Pour soup mixture on top. Sprinkle cheese over soup mixture.

In a small saucepan or microwave melt ¼ c. butter. Toss in bread cubes and mix well. Layer bread cubes on top of cheese. Bake for 20-30 minutes until heated through.

Notes

Chicken Nancy

I have no idea where this recipe came from, but the sherry just brings everything together.

- 4 boneless, chicken breasts
- 4 pieces of swiss cheese
- 1 can cream of chicken or mushroom soup
- ½ c. sherry
- 2 c. herb crouton stuffing
- ½ c. (1 stick) butter, melted

Preheat oven to 350°. Arrange chicken breasts in a casserole dish and cover each breast with a slice of cheese. In a small bowl, mix together soup and sherry. Pour over chicken breasts. Top with stuffing and drizzle butter over all. Bake at 350° for 1½ hours or until done.

Notes

Chicken and Orange Biscuits

This is one of my favorite recipes that my mother made while I was growing up. My kids now love it too. I have adapted it a bit by cutting the chicken in pieces, but the original recipe called for 4 whole breasts. It's great served over rice!

- 1 pkg. buttermilk biscuits (dough)
- 4 boneless, skinless chicken breasts, cut into small pieces
- flour
- salt and pepper
- ½ c. butter

Orange Sauce:

- 1 c. orange juice
- 1 t. orange peel
- 1 T. lemon juice
- ½ c. sugar
- 1 T. cornstarch
- 2 T. butter

Melt butter in a 9"x13" pan. Dip chicken in flour, salt and pepper. (I like to place a little flour, salt and pepper in a large plastic bag and add pieces of chicken and shake until covered.) Place chicken in pan and coat with melted butter. Bake at 375° for about 20 minutes. Stir and bake a few minutes more until almost done. Remove pan from oven, push pieces to side of pan. On cleared side place biscuits side by side. Pour orange sauce over all. Bake according to directions on roll package.

Serves about 4.

Notes

Chicken Noodle Soup

My grandmother used to make the best egg noodles. She cooked them in broth she had made from baking a roast. I love to put them in chicken noodle soup. They taste incredible and are such a comfort food! Whenever I have sick kids, this is the perfect remedy! It takes a bit of time, perfect to make on a Sunday afternoon and then you can also freeze it in portions to have at a later time.

Chicken Stock:
- 1 whole chicken about 3½ pounds, rinsed
- 1 small pkg. ready to eat baby carrots
- 2 celery stalks, chopped
- 2 lg. onions, chopped
- 1 head of garlic, halved
- 2 turnips, chopped
- 1 T. thyme
- 1 T. Herbs of Provence
- 2 bay leaves
- 1 T. whole black peppercorns

Soup:
- 2 T. butter or olive oil
- 1 lg. onion, chopped
- 4 garlic cloves, minced
- 1 small pkg. ready to eat baby carrots
- 1 celery stalk, chopped
- 3 T. chicken bouillon

Notes

Chicken Noodle Soup Continued

Noodles:

- 2 c. flour
- 1 t. baking powder
- 1 t. salt
- 5 eggs, beaten

To make stock:

Place all ingredients in a large pot. Cover with water. Bring to a boil and then simmer for 1-2 hours until chicken is done. Remove chicken, discard skin and bones, chop chicken and set aside. Strain stock through a colander, discard vegetables (yes, really). At this point you can refrigerate stock until ready to use. It lasts about a week or you can freeze it.

To make soup:

Melt butter/heat oil in a large pot. Add garlic and onion. Add remaining soup ingredients. Cook for about 10 minutes. Pour in chicken stock and bring to a boil. Simmer for 30 minutes or until vegetables are tender. Season with salt and pepper. Add noodles and cook until tender (about 5 minutes).

To make noodles:

In a large bowl, mix dry ingredients. Blend in eggs and mix until just blended. Roll out onto a well floured surface to about ¼" thick. Sprinkle lots of flour on top. Cut into small strips (you can use a pizza cutter). Drop into hot broth and cook until tender.

Notes

Chicken with Brie and Basil Sauce

This one is quick, easy and tastes like you spent all day in the kitchen. Fresh basil for the sauce is a must!

- 5 boneless, skinless chicken breasts
- salt and pepper
- 4 T. olive oil
- 1 T. oregano
- 1 T. dried basil
- 3 garlic cloved, minced
- 3 T. pine nuts
- 12 oz. brie
- 2 c. fresh tomatoes
- 2 T. fresh parsley
- 6 large fresh basil leaves, chopped
- 8 oz bow tie pasta or any other kind desired

Cut chicken into small bite-sized pieces. Place 2 T. oil in a medium skillet. Add 1 minced garlic clove. Add chicken, oregano and dried basil. Cook until chicken is browned and done. Place in a serving dish and keep warm until sauce is finished. In a small ungreased pan, toast pine nuts until they are golden brown, do not burn as they will make the entire dish bitter. Set aside. Cook pasta according to directions, set aside. Cut the rind off of the brie and scrape brie until most of the white rind is gone. In a large frying pan, heat 2 T. olive oil. Add tomato, garlic, parsley and basil. Sauté for about 1 minute. Add brie and toasted pine nuts. Cook over low heat and slowly stir until the cheese is completely melted. Pour sauce over chicken and bow tie pasta and serve immediately.

Serves 4-6.

Notes

Col. Culling's Yaki-Mandu (Korean Egg Rolls)

In 1976, my dad was stationed in Korea with his friend Mike Green. They met up years later again when we lived in Chicago, Illinois. We had these wonderful egg rolls at his house for dinner. He gave the recipe to my dad. It dawned on me not too long ago that they aren't authentic as the recipe calls for Monterey Jack Cheese. Regardless, they are absolutely delicious. I learned how to make them when I was in 6th grade and I've been making them ever since.

- 1 lb. hamburger
- 1 lb. hot sausage (I use Jimmy Dean's hot sausage)
- 2 c. green onions, sliced (not too thin about ¼ inch slices)
- 2 c. Monterey Jack cheese, shredded
- 2 pkg. small egg roll wraps (bring them to room temperature or they will crack when you roll them)
- 2 eggs

Brown hamburger and sausage together until just lightly brown. Drain meat in a colander and wipe out pan. Return browned meat to pan. Add green onions and cheese. Heat on low until cheese is just melted. Turn off heat.

Beat eggs in a small bowl. Take egg roll wrappers out of package and place on a large cutting board. Place a damp paper towel over wrappers while you work.

Place a wrapper on the cutting board, with a point side toward you. Spoon about ½ T. of meat mixture into the center of the wrapper. Dip finger into egg and spread it onto opposite

Notes

Col. Culling's Yaki-Mandu (Korean Egg Rolls) Continued

triangle of wrapper. Roll up egg roll about half-way and pull in edges, continue rolling and seal outside of point with more beaten egg. Place on a cookie sheet lined with parchment paper. Place a damp paper towel over the top so the egg rolls do not dry out. Refrigerate until you are ready to fry them (do not leave in refrigerator more than 1 day). Although I think they are best the same day, you can also freeze them. Flash freeze them on the cookie sheet and then transfer to a ziplock bag. When you're ready to use them, thaw them out slightly before frying them.

To fry:

Heat deep fryer or oil in a pan on stove to about 375°. Deep fry until golden brown. Drain on paper towels and serve with a side dish of soy sauce.

Makes about 96 small egg rolls.

Notes

Easy Pork Tenderloin

I have other tenderloin recipes but this one is the easiest by far. And when I'm in a hurry, this is the one I use.

- whole tenderloin
- lemon pepper
- garlic salt
- 3 slices of bacon

Preheat oven to 350°. Sprinkle tenderloin with lemon pepper and garlic salt. Lay slices of bacon across. Bake for about 40 minutes or until thermometer registers 165° when inserted.

Notes

Fried Chicken

I have searched high and low for great fried chicken. This recipe is a combination of a few recipes I've found. It's not hard but it does take 2-3 days if you want the best results. Of course it's not healthy at all, but it sure tastes great and it's worth it when you want to splurge!

- 1 1b. chicken – you can cut up boneless breasts to make chicken nuggets/fingers, or buy drumsticks, legs, thighs – whatever you prefer
- 2 T. salt
- buttermilk
- 2 T. tabasco
- 1½ c. self-rising flour
- 2 T. seasoning salt
- 1 t. black pepper
- 2 eggs, beaten
- vegetable oil

Place chicken in a large bowl. Cover with water. Add 2 T. salt. Refrigerate at least 4 hours or overnight. Drain well. Cover chicken with buttermilk, place plastic wrap over top and soak again for at least a few hours or again overnight. Pour chicken in a colander and drain off buttermilk. In a large bowl, or zip top bag, mix flour, seasoning salt, and pepper. In a separate bowl, mix eggs, Tabasco, and ½ c. buttermilk. Coat chicken with flour mixture. Dip into egg mixture and back again into flour mixture. Depending on

Notes

Fried Chicken Continued

whether you use chicken pieces, breasts or legs, you may need more or less flour and egg mixture.

Deep fry chicken in oil in a fryer or on the stove. Cook until chicken is done and outside is a deep golden brown.

Serve with ranch dressing, barbeque sauce or just alone. These make great appetizers if you make "chicken nuggets."

Notes

Granny's Meatloaf

My grandmother made an excellent meat loaf. Over the years I have added a few ingredients to make it even better. She would be proud!

- 2 large onions, finely chopped
- 1 c. celery, finely chopped
- 2 cloves garlic, minced
- 2 T. butter
- 2 t. salt
- 2 t. pepper
- 2 t. Worcestershire sauce
- ⅔ c. ketchup
- 1½ lb. ground beef
- 1 lb. hot ground pork sausage (I use Jimmy Dean)
- 1 c. oatmeal
- 2 large eggs, beaten
- ⅓ c. kale, chopped finely
- 3 slices of bacon

Preheat oven to 350°. In a large skillet, melt butter. Add onions, celery, and garlic. Sauté until vegetables are tender. In a large mixing bowl, combine ground beef, sausage, eggs, vegetables, salt and pepper, Worcestershire sauce, ⅓ c. ketchup, oatmeal and kale. Form into a loaf and place in a 9"x13" baking pan. Cover with remaining ketchup and place 3 strips of bacon across the loaf. Bake meatloaf for about 45-60 minutes or until done.

Serves 6-8.

Notes

Indian Pot Roast

I found this recipe for my mom when I was in the 6th grade. My mom used to make roast every Sunday and it was a nice variation from the norm. This one is very simple, but delicious! Definitely make the dumplings. They're worth it!

- 3-4 lb. pot roast
- 3 cloves garlic, minced
- 6 T. butter, divided
- salt
- flour
- 2 lg onions sliced
- 2 T. pepper corns
- 2 t. allspice
- 1 bay leaf, crumbled
- 2 T. horseradish
- ¾ c. red wine
- ¼ c. water

Dumplings:
- 2 c. flour
- 4 t. baking powder
- ½ t. salt
- 1 scant cup of milk

Sauté minced garlic in 2 T. butter in a large pot or Dutch oven. Rub meat with salt and flour. Brown roast in the garlic butter well on all sides. Lay meat on a bed of thinly

Notes

Indian Pot Roast Continued

sliced onions in a Dutch oven, or large pan covered tightly with foil. Add 4 T. butter, spices and pour wine over meat. As it cooks pour ¼ c. water over roast. Cover tightly and simmer 3-4 hours until tender (in oven 325° for about 2-3 hours). Add carrots the last 30 minutes of cooking and add dumplings the last 12 minutes.

To make dumplings:

Sift together flour, baking powder and salt. Gradually add milk. Drop by spoonfuls onto gravy and cook last 12 minutes of roast time.

Serves 6-8.

Notes

Jäger Schnitzel

I was born in Germany and later spent two of my college years there. Jäger Schnitzel is still my favorite German dish to this day. Unfortunately I never watched anyone make it so I've had to piece together recipes over the years and come up with my own version of it. It's really a version of Jäger and Rahm-schnitzel. This is excellent served with German Spätzle noodles, or use my egg noodle recipe found in this book (page 73).

- 4-6 boneless pork chops
- salt and pepper
- flour
- 2 T. butter
- ½ c. onion, chopped
- 2 c. red wine
- ¾ c. beef broth
- 1 garlic clove, minced
- ½ t. dried thyme or use fresh
- 1 c. mushrooms, sliced thin
- 3 T. sour cream or heavy cream

Pound out meat into thin pieces using a meat mallet. Season with salt and pepper. Dip pork pieces into flour. In a heavy pan, heat oil. Sear both sides of pork until golden. Remove from heat and set aside. Add butter, onion, garlic, thyme and mushrooms. Sauté for about 3 minutes. Add wine and cook until reduced by about half. Add beef broth and return meat

Notes

Jäger Schnitzel Continued

to pan. Simmer on low and cook until meat is tender. Transfer meat to a plate and keep warm. Add sour cream to skillet. Cook for a bit until it turns into a creamy sauce. Pour this on top of the pork and serve with noodles.

Serves 4-6.

Notes

Mom's Beer Chili

My mom has been making this chili since I was little. The original recipe came from a newspaper clipping but we can't remember where!

- 2 T. butter
- 4 lb. round steak
- ½ c. flour or more
- 2 16 oz. cans of stewed tomatoes
- 2 pkg. Williams chili seasoning, I can't find it in California, so I just use whatever I can find
- 1 small can of mushrooms or you can use fresh (I use about 1 c. fresh mushrooms)
- 1 16 oz. can corn
- 1 T. salt
- 1½ t. pepper
- 2 t. cumin
- 3 cloves garlic, minced
- 3 large onions, chopped
- 2 green peppers, chopped
- 2 red peppers, chopped
- ½ t. red pepper flakes
- 2 T. parsley flakes, or fresh
- 3-4 cans red kidney beans
- 4 bay leaves

Notes

Mom's Beer Chili Continued

- 4 cans/bottles of beer (some people substitute water, but I like the beer)

Toppings:

- Fritos
- sharp cheddar cheese
- sour cream
- hot sauce/hot salsa, if desired

Cut up the round steak into small 1 inch pieces. Shake the pieces of meat in a zip top bag with the flour. Use more flour if needed to coat the pieces well. Brown the coated meat in the butter in a large skillet, or I like to divide the meat and brown it between 2 large soup pots and save myself from washing an extra skillet. (When I make this chili, I use 2 pots as I don't have a pot large enough for the batch. I divide the ingredients evenly between the two pots). After the meat is browned, add 3 cans of beer. Add the remaining ingredients including spices. If there is not a "free flow" of chili, add more beer/water until there is. Cook on low heat for 4 hours, stirring every 30 minutes or so. It's best made the day before and can be frozen.

When serving, place a handful of Fritos in the bowl, add the chili and then a handful of sharp cheddar cheese and a dollop of sour cream. If you like it spicier, add a bit of hot sauce or hot salsa.

Makes enough chili for at least 10-12 people if not more!

Notes

Puffy Pancakes

I have had this recipe since I was in the 8th grade. I lived in Naperville, Illinois and I received this recipe in my home economics class. It's fun to watch the pancakes rise. They fall pretty quickly when out of the oven, but they taste great!

- ½ c. butter (one stick)
- 1 c. flour
- 6 eggs
- 1 c. milk
- ¼ c. orange juice
- ½ c. sugar
- ¼ t. salt
- 1 t. vanilla
- pinch of nutmeg

Preheat oven to 425°. Melt butter in a 9"x13" pan, just until melted. Using a blender, blend remaining ingredients until well blended. Quickly pour the mixture evenly into the pie plate. Mix batter with butter. Bake for 15-20 minutes until puffed and light brown. Cut into slices and serve with hot maple syrup.

Serves 8.

Notes

Quick and Easy Fajita Marinade

I love to spend time making marinades, but sometimes, you just need one in a hurry and this one is it!

- ¼ c. oil (The original recipe called for ½ c. but I don't really think you need that much.)
- ⅓ c. lime juice
- 2 pkg. Hidden Valley Ranch dressing mix
- 1 t. cumin
- ½ t. black pepper

Combine all ingredients together and pour over 2 pounds of steak or chicken breasts. Refrigerate overnight. Grill and cut diagonally. This one really tastes best if done overnight.

Notes

Scrambled Eggs with Brown Rice and Kale

Even though most of the recipes in this cookbook are calorie-laden, I don't actually eat heavy meals every day. In fact I almost always start my day with a version of this recipe.

- 2 t. olive oil (I also use a non-stick pan)
- 1 garlic clove, optional
- 1 T. chopped onion or leek
- 3 fresh mushrooms, chopped
- 1 egg
- 2 egg whites
- 2-3 cups of kale or swiss chard, chopped
- ½ c. brown rice, cooked (Because I eat a version of this almost every day, I cook a big batch of rice in a rice cooker typically on Mondays and then refrigerate the rest for the remaining days).

Brown onions, garlic and mushrooms in 2 t. oil. Add chopped kale/swiss chard. Brown lightly, then turn heat on low. In the meantime, beat eggs in a small bowl with a fork. Add beaten eggs to kale and onion mixture. Turn heat on medium and cook until eggs are almost done. Add brown rice and cook until everything is heated through. Enjoy!

This recipe makes enough for 2 people. Pair this with a Zhen Qu which is a Yunnan tea and you have an outstanding combination!

Variations:

Notes

Scrambled Eggs with Brown Rice and Kale Continued

- Try adding salsa and tomatoes
- Try adding parmesan cheese (just a wee bit if you want the recipe to stay healthy)
- Try adding black beans

The possibilities are endless. I find it's the perfect amount of protein and the right kind of carbs. It gets me through until snack time.

Notes

Spinach Casserole

This recipe came from my mother's childhood friend. She is an excellent cook!

- 2 pkg. frozen chopped spinach
- 1 8 oz. pkg. cream cheese, softened
- 2 T. horseradish
- 1 c. sour cream
- 6 slices of bacon, fried and crumbled
- 1 c. stuffing mix
- ¼ c. (½ stick) butter, melted
- salt

Cook spinach according to package directions. Drain. Blend in cream cheese. Add horseradish, sour cream, bacon and salt to taste. Mix well. Place in a greased casserole dish. Mix stuffing with melted butter. Sprinkle on top of spinach mixture. Bake for 20-30 minutes at 350°. Casserole may be assembled and refrigerated overnight. Add bacon and top with stuffing just before baking.

Serves 6.

Notes

Taco Salad

This recipe is an old one and came from the Midwest. I find that many people do not use Velveeta anymore. To lighten this one up a bit, just use shredded cheddar cheese instead of the Velveeta.

- 1½ lb. ground beef
- 1 c. green pepper, finely chopped
- ½ c. onions, finely chopped
- 4 t. chili powder
- ⅛ t. cumin powder
- 1 lb. Velveeta cheese
- 1 10 oz. can tomatoes and green chilies
- 1 head of lettuce, any kind
- 2 tomatoes, chopped
- 1 bag of Fritos

Brown ground beef with green pepper and onion. Drain well. Add tomatoes and green chilies. Add spices. Melt cheese in a double boiler or in a microwave. Tear lettuce in a large bowl, add tomatoes and Fritos. Add hot meat mixture. Add melted cheese. Toss well and serve right away. Unfortunately this salad does not do well as left-overs.

Serves 6.

Notes

Tuna Casserole

My mom used to make this weekly during Lent. I've made a few additions to make it creamier.

- 1 can tuna, well-drained
- 1 can cream of mushroom soup
- 1 8 oz. pkg. cream cheese
- ¼ c. onion, finely chopped
- 2 c. uncooked macaroni

Preheat oven to 350°. Bring water to boil in a medium saucepan. Add macaroni. Cook for about 7 minutes or until tender. Drain well. In a medium bowl, mix tuna, mushroom soup, cream cheese and onions. Mix in macaroni. Place in a greased 9"x13" dish and bake for about 30 minutes.

Notes

Wiener Schnitzel

I finally figured out the secret to the crispiness. Make sure you let the breading refrigerate for at least an hour before frying them. They are great with a side dish and a salad. They also make a nice tenderloin sandwich with onions, mustard and cucumber slices on a toasted bun.

- 4-6 boneless pork chops
- salt and pepper
- flour
- bread crumbs or crushed crackers
- 2 eggs, beaten
- vegetable oil

Pound out meat into thin pieces using a meat mallet. Season with salt and pepper. Beat eggs in a small dish. Dip pork pieces into flour, then eggs, then breadcrumbs or cracker crumbs. Place the dipped pieces on a platter, separate with waxed paper or parchment paper. Cover with plastic wrap and chill for at least one hour. This allows the breading to "set."

When ready to eat, heat oil in a large frying pan to about 350°. Fry schnitzel for about 1½ minutes on each side or until golden brown. Drain on paper towels and keep warm until ready to serve. These are best eaten right away. Squeeze lemon over the top just before serving.

Notes

Desserts

Amaretto Fruit Dip

This recipe is great to serve in the summer. If you need to store it for a day or so, make up the pudding and store it separately, then add the whipped topping and amaretto right before you serve it.

- 1 small box vanilla pudding
- milk
- ¾ c. amaretto (see recipe on page 171)
- 1 small container of whipped topping (Cool Whip)

Make up pudding according to pudding directions. Cool. Blend in amaretto. Lightly fold in whipped topping. Be careful not to stir too much.

Serve with fresh fruit.

Notes

Apple Dumplings

I like to make big batches of these during the fall apple season and then freeze them for later. When you want a fabulous dessert, just make up the sauce and bake the apples.

- 2 c. flour
- 2 t. baking powder
- 1 t. salt
- ⅔ c. shortening
- ½ c. milk
- additional cinnamon and sugar
- nutmeg
- about 2 T. butter, cut into small cubes
- 6 apples

Sauce:
- 1½ c. sugar
- 1½ c. water
- ¼ t. cinnamon
- ¼ t. nutmeg
- 3 T. butter

In a medium bowl, sift together flour, baking powder and salt. Cut in shortening with a pastry cutter. Add milk and stir until just moistened. Roll out dough ¼ inch thick into a 18"x12" rectangle. Cut into 6 inch squares. Peel and core apples. Place cored and peeled apple in center of square. Sprinkle apple with a little cinnamon, sugar and nutmeg.

Notes

Apple Dumplings Continued

Dot with butter. Moisten edges of squares, fold in corners to center and pinch edges. (Or I like to form the dough around the apple so they looked like dough-covered apples). At this point you can freeze the apple. When ready to bake, place each apple about 1 inch apart on a greased 11"x7" pan. Pour sauce over apples. Sprinkle with additional sugar. Bake at 375° for 35 minutes or until apples are done and tender in the center.

To make sauce:

Combine sugar, water, cinnamon and nutmeg in a saucepan. Bring to a boil. Remove from heat. Add butter.

Serve with a scoop of vanilla ice cream.

Notes

Aunt Janet's Coffee Cake

In May of 2009, my cousin was married at a beautiful resort in Tennessee. We all stayed in a huge cabin that overlooked the Smokey Mountains. For breakfast my aunt made this coffee cake. It's absolutely delicious! You can't eat just one piece!

- 1 box yellow cake mix
- 1 small box of vanilla instant pudding
- ¾ c. vegetable oil
- ¾ c. water
- 4 eggs
- 1 T. butter extract (I could never find this, so I leave it out)
- 1 T. vanilla
- ½ c. sugar
- 2 T. cinnamon

Topping:
- 1 c. powdered sugar
- 1 T. hot milk
- ½ t. butter extract
- ¼ t. vanilla

Preheat oven to 350°. Butter/grease a 9"x13" pan. Beat cake mix, pudding, water, eggs and oil for about 8 minutes on medium speed. Add butter extract and vanilla. Pour half of mixture in the buttered pan. Mix ½ c. sugar and 2 T. cinnamon. Sprinkle half mixture over batter in pan. Spread rest of batter on top and then the rest of sugar mixture on top. Swirl knife throughout cake. Bake for 30-35 minutes. Mix together topping ingredients. Drizzle over hot cake.

Notes

Banana Cake with Caramel Frosting

The caramel sugar icing is what makes this cake outstanding. If you're looking for a sugar high, this is it! I have spent hours trying to recreate this recipe as my grandmother made it. Although I do have her original recipe, she loved to cook without a recipe so when she did write one down for you, she often forgot to write down all of the ingredients, or she would not put a measurement for the ingredient. Her banana cake had a semi-hard sugar icing which you could break off easily. This is my version of the cake, not exactly like hers, but close. It's absolutely fantastic!

- 2 c. flour
- 1 t. baking soda
- 1 t. baking powder
- ½ t. salt
- ¾ c. shortening/butter
- 1 c. sugar
- ½ c. brown sugar
- 2 eggs
- 1 t. vanilla
- 3 medium bananas, mashed
- ½ c. buttermilk

Icing:
- 1 c. butter
- 3 c. brown sugar
- 6 T. milk

Notes

Banana Cake with Caramel Frosting Continued

- 1 t. vanilla

Preheat oven to 375°. Mix flour, soda, baking powder and salt together. Set aside. With a mixer, cream shortening/butter and sugar together until light and fluffy. Add eggs, bananas and vanilla. Beat for about 2 minutes. Add flour mixture to creamed mixture alternately with buttermilk, beat well after each addition ending with flour mixture. Pour into a greased 9"x13" pan. Bake for about 25 minutes or until done in center when a toothpick is inserted. Cool while making icing.

To make icing:

Place butter, brown sugar and milk in a medium heavy weight saucepan. Bring to a full boil on medium heat for about four minutes stirring frequently. Turn off heat. Add 1 teaspoon vanilla. Set timer for 10 minutes and allow to cool, but stir frequently. After 10 minutes, stir constantly (still with heat off) for about 3 more minutes. Pour over cake and allow icing to set. (Note: As it cools, the icing will thicken. You'll see the texture change from buttery liquid after you take it off the heat, to thin caramel liquid to eventually a thicker melted chocolate consistency.) When the mixture starts to take on a duller sheen and thicken up slightly, you'll know it's time to pour it over the cake. Once you pour it on, it starts to set immediately. Don't wait too long or it will harden up. If that happens, put it back over the heat for just a bit, add a few tablespoons of milk if necessary, stir and pour over cake. Let cake set for a few hours before serving. Store in the refrigerator.

Notes

Choc Bars

When I was in college in Munich, Germany, I had a part-time job at the university office as a receptionist. One day a co-worker brought in these goodies. I practically ate the whole plate by myself! This is my favorite recipe to take to a party when I need a great dessert. I always get rave reviews on it. We did serve this at the tea room but it needed a more dignified name, so I renamed them, "Chocolate Oatmeal Delights".

- 1 c. butter
- 2 c. brown sugar
- 2 eggs
- 2½ c. flour
- 1 t. salt
- 1 t. baking soda
- 3 c. oatmeal
- 12 oz. semisweet chocolate chips
- 1 can sweetened condensed milk
- 2 T. butter

Cream together 1 c. butter, brown sugar and eggs. Sift together flour, salt and baking soda. Add to creamed mixture. Stir in oatmeal. Press ¾ of mixture into a 9"x13" pan. (Reserve the remaining ¼ mixture.) Melt together chocolate chips, sweetened condensed milk and 2 T. butter. Pour over oatmeal mixture. Crumble/chunk the reserved oatmeal mixture on the top of the chocolate mixture. Bake at 350° for 20 minutes. Do not over-bake.

Let set for a few hours before cutting.

Notes

Chocolate Cream Pie

This was one of my grandmother's recipes. My kids absolutely adore this one!

- ¾ c. sugar
- ⅓ c. flour
- ¼ t. salt
- 2 c. milk
- 2 eggs
- 1 T. butter
- ½ c. semi sweet chocolate chips
- 1 t. vanilla
- 1 baked and cooled pie shell

In a sauce pan mix sugar, flour and salt. Add 1 c. of milk; mix until smooth. Bring to boil over medium heat, stirring briskly. Continue to stir and boil until thickened, about 2 minutes. Remove from heat. With a fork, beat eggs with remaining 1 c. of milk; gradually stir into hot mixture, then put back over heat. Bring to a boil, stirring and continue boiling until mixture thickens a bit more, about 1 minute. Remove from heat, stir in butter, chocolate and vanilla. Stir until chocolate is melted. Pour into pie shell. Chill.

Notes

Double Rum Cake

This is a combination of two of my favorite rum cakes. It's super easy, and everyone loves it. It actually tastes better the next day. For a smoother cake texture, omit the coconut.

- 1 18.5 oz. pkg. yellow cake mix (I use Duncan Hines Moist Deluxe Butter Recipe Mix)
- 1 3½ oz. pkg. instant vanilla pudding mix
- ½ c. sweetened coconut, optional
- ½ c. spiced rum or regular rum
- ½ c. vegetable oil
- ½ c. water
- 4 eggs
- ¾ c. chopped pecans, optional

Rum Sauce:

- 1 c. sugar
- ¼ c. butter
- ¼ c. spiced rum
- dash of water

Preheat the oven to 325°. Spray a non-stick 2 qt. Bundt pan with cooking spray. Using an electric mixer at low speed, blend the cake mix, pudding mix, coconut, rum, oil and ½ c. water. Add eggs, one at a time beating well after each addition.

Evenly distribute the pecans in the bottom of the Bundt pan. Pour the batter on top of the pecans. Bake for 50-55 minutes,

Notes

Double Rum Cake Continued

or until a knife comes out clean.

To make the rum sauce:

In a small saucepan, bring the sugar, butter, rum and dash of water to a boil and cook for 3 minutes. With a fork, make holes in the top of the cake. Pour half of the sauce over the cake and let sit for 10 minutes.

Invert pan onto a serving plate. Pour the other half of the sauce over the top of cake.

Serve when cooled.

Notes

Four Layer German Chocolate Cake

My grandmother always made this cake for my mom's birthday, the day after Christmas. Because she lived in Missouri, she used to store the cake on her cold back porch. I remember one year she accidentally dropped the cake when bringing it in. She just told me, "Shh! We won't tell anyone." She put it back together and no one ever knew anything but the two of us. After making this cake, I can certainly see why we just put it back together. It does take a while to make, but the results are worth it! Because of the 4 layers it makes quite a statement. Be prepared to eat cake!

- 8 oz. sweet dark chocolate, melted and cooled
- 4⅔ c. cake flour
- 3 c. sugar
- 2 t. baking soda
- 1 t. baking powder
- 1 t. salt
- 1⅓ c. butter, softened
- 2 c. buttermilk, divided
- 2 t. vanilla
- 4 eggs

Frosting:

- 2 c. sugar
- 8 egg yolks
- 2 c. evaporated milk

Notes

Four Layer German Chocolate Cake Continued

- 1 c. butter
- 2 t. vanilla
- 20 oz. sweetened coconut
- 3 c. pecans, finely chopped
- ½ c. warm milk (to thin frosting if needed, I use the left-over evaporated milk if needed)

Grease and flour four 9 inch cake pans (or use flour spray). In a small bowl, mix together flour, sugar, baking soda, baking powder and salt. In a mixing bowl, cream butter; add flour mixture, 1½ c. buttermilk and vanilla. Mix on low just until dry ingredients are moistened. Then beat at medium speed for 2 minutes – scrape sides often. Add melted chocolate, eggs, and remaining ½ c. buttermilk. Pour batter into prepared cake pans. Bake for about 25-35 minutes or until done when a toothpick is inserted and comes out clean. Cool in pans for 15 minutes. Run a knife around edge of cake, invert and cool completely on wire racks.

To make frosting:

Combine sugar, egg yolks, and evaporated milk in a non-stick saucepan. Stir with a wire whisk until the yolks are fully incorporated. Place over medium heat, add the butter. Constantly stir until mixture come to a boil. Continue cooking until mixture thickens about 10 minutes. Turn off heat. Add vanilla, coconut and nuts. Add extra warm milk if needed to thin frosting a bit. Cool.

Notes

Four Layer German Chocolate Cake Continued

To assemble:

Place one layer on a cake stand or plate and spread with frosting. Frost each layer completely before adding next layer. Place in refrigerator and allow to set a bit before cutting. Store in refrigerator.

Notes

Fruit Pizza

This is a beautiful dessert! When you alternate fruit pieces around the cookie, it looks very professional, even if you aren't an artist! Look at mine on the front cover and I'm definitely not artistic by nature.

- 2 pkg. refrigerated sugar cookie dough
- 1 8 oz. pkg. cream cheese, softened
- ¼ c. powdered sugar
- 1 t. vanilla
- various different kinds of fruit – blueberries, raspberries, grapes, mandarin orange segments, kiwi, etc.

Spray a pizza pan with non-stick spray. Slice cookie dough into thin slices and overlap slices to cover entire pizza pan. Press slices together lightly. Bake at 375° for about 12 minutes or until lightly browned. Cool.

In a small bowl, beat together cream cheese, powdered sugar and vanilla until smooth. Spread over cooled cookie dough. Wash and drain fruit very well. Blot fruit with a paper towel. Arrange fruit on top of the cream cheese mixture. It looks best if you start on the outside of the circle and alternate fruit around, then do the next circle inside, each time alternating fruit. Example: blueberry, grape, blueberry all around the outside, then mandarin orange segment, raspberry, mandarin orange segment, etc. then in the middle have a kiwi, etc.

Be creative, it really doesn't matter what fruit you use, just alternate each piece and it will turn out

Notes

Fruit Pizza Continued

beautifully.

When finished, if desired, coat with a glaze of orange marmalade diluted with water. If you don't use fruits which turn brown, such as apples or bananas, you don't need the glaze.

Cut into pizza slices and serve. This does look best when made early in the day and served later. You can make it the day before, but the fruit doesn't look as nice. My advice if you need to prepare it ahead of time: make up the creamed cheese mixture and store in refrigerator, bake the pizza cookie, cool and cover with plastic wrap. Wash fruit and drain it well. Then put it all together the day of the event.

Notes

Homemade Banana Pudding

I love homemade banana pudding and I was a bit frantic when I lost my favorite recipe for a while. I finally found it while working on this cookbook. It really it doesn't take that much more time than instant pudding and it's so worth the effort. You'll be glad you did!

- 2 c. sugar
- 3 T. self rising flour
- 3 egg yolks
- 3½ c. milk
- 1½ tsp. vanilla
- ¼ c. butter (½ stick)
- 3-4 medium bananas
- 1 box of vanilla wafers (I like to buy the mini wafers and serve the pudding in custard cups)

In a non-stick saucepan, mix together flour and sugar. Gradually add in milk and beaten egg yolks. Cook over medium heat stirring until it thickens. Remember to keep stirring or pudding will burn and become lumpy. When pudding has thickened (it should coat the back of a wooden spoon), turn off heat. Add butter and vanilla.

In a 9"x13" pan or custard cups, place vanilla wafers on bottom. Add sliced bananas over wafers. Pour pudding on top. Cool in refrigerator until set, then serve.

Notes

Jamaican Banana Bread

This recipe was the inspiration for the Jamaican Scones we made at the tea room.

- 2 T. butter, softened
- 2 T. cream cheese, softened
- 1 c. sugar
- 1 egg
- 2 c. flour
- 2 t. baking powder
- ½ t. baking soda
- ⅛ t. salt
- 1 c. banana, ripe and mashed
- ½ c. milk
- 2 T. rum
- 1 t. grated lime rind
- 2 t. lime juice
- 1 t. vanilla
- ¼ c. pecans, toasted
- ¼ c. sweetened coconut

Topping:
- ½ c. dark brown sugar
- 4 t. butter
- 4 t. lime juice
- 4 t. rum

Notes

Jamaican Banana Bread Continued

- 4 T. pecan, toasted, chopped
- 4 T. sweetened coconut

Preheat oven to 375°. Spray a loaf pan with cooking spray. In a mixing bowl, beat 2 T. butter, cream cheese, and 1 c. sugar. Add egg. Beat well. In a small bowl, combine flour, baking powder, baking soda and salt. In another bowl combine banana, milk, rum, lime rind, lime juice and vanilla. Add flour mixture to creamed mixture alternately with banana mixture, beginning and ending with flour mixture. Stir in ¼ c. pecans and ¼ c. coconut. Pour into loaf pan and bake for 50-60 minutes or until done. Let cool in pan for 10 minutes. Run a knife around loaf before removing and place on a wire rack to cool.

To make topping:

Combine brown sugar, butter, lime juice and rum in a small saucepan. Cook for about 2 minutes and then add coconut and pecans. Pour over banana loaf.

This recipe works well as muffins. You'll probably need to double the topping recipe however.

Notes

Kahlua Cake

This recipe came from a neighbor we were stationed with in Neu Ulm, Germany. She always had great recipes!

- 1 box of yellow cake mix
- 1 small box instant chocolate pudding
- 1 c. oil
- 4 eggs
- ¾ c. orange juice
- ½ c. Kahlua

Preheat oven to 350°. In a large mixing bowl combine all ingredients. Pour into a Bundt pan. Bake at 350° for about 50-60 minutes or until done.

Notes

Mom's Chocolate Sheet Cake

My mother used to make this every year for my birthday. It has a crunchy chocolate icing when set. It's a fairly quick cake to make and you pour the frosting on hot. You don't have to put nuts in the frosting, but it definitely tastes better if you do!

Cake:
- 1 c. sugar
- 1 c. flour
- ¼ t. salt
- ½ c. butter
- 1½ T. cocoa
- ½ c. water
- 1 egg, beaten
- ¼ c. buttermilk
- ½ t. baking soda
- ½ t. vanilla

Icing:
- ¼ c. butter
- 3 T. milk
- 1 T. cocoa
- ½ t. vanilla
- ½ lb. powdered sugar
- ½ c. pecans

Notes

Mom's Chocolate Sheet Cake Continued

Mix sugar, flour and salt in a large bowl. Set aside. In a saucepan, bring ½ c. butter, 1½ T. cocoa and water to a rapid boil. Pour over sugar/flour mixture. Mix well. In a separate bowl, mix egg, buttermilk, baking soda and vanilla. Add mixture to flour mixture. Pour into a greased 9"x13" pan. Bake at 400° for about 20 minutes. Reduce heat to 375° and bake until done, have icing ready when cake comes out of the oven.

To make icing:

Bring butter, milk and cocoa to a boil. Turn off heat. Add powdered sugar and vanilla. Beat until smooth. Add pecans and spread on cake while hot. Let set.

Serve when cool.

Notes

Pumpkin Cake

My kids adore this dessert warm, but I actually think it tastes better after it's been in the refrigerator for a few hours.

- 3 eggs
- 1 15 oz. can pumpkin
- 1 12 oz can evaporated milk
- 1 c. sugar
- ⅛ t. salt
- 1 ½ t. cinnamon
- 1 t. ginger
- 1 T. vanilla extract
- 1 18.25 oz box yellow cake mix
- 1¼ c. butter, melted
- 1 c. chopped nuts, pecans are wonderful

Preheat oven to 350°. Mix together first 8 ingredients. Pour into a 9"x13" ungreased baking dish. Sprinkle cake mix on top. Do not stir. (Yes, really!) Drizzle with melted butter. Bake at 350° for 25 minutes. Top with nuts and bake another 15 minutes or until firm.

Serve hot or cold. Scoop into dishes and top with whipped cream.

Notes

Special K Cookies

My grandmother always spoiled me, as grandmothers do! She let me eat these for breakfast as they had "cereal" in them.

- 1 c. brown sugar
- 1 c. sugar
- 1 c. oil
- ½ c. butter, softened
- 2 eggs
- 1 t. vanilla
- ½ c. nuts
- 2 c. flour
- 2 c. oatmeal
- 2 c. Special K cereal
- 1 t. baking soda
- ½ t. baking powder
- ¼ t. salt

Preheat oven to 325°. Mix all ingredients and drop by teaspoonfuls onto a cookie sheet. Bake at 325° for about 10 minutes or until done.

Makes about 3½ dozen.

These are thin, flat and lacy cookies, if you want them more traditionally shaped, then put the dough in the refrigerator for a little while before dropping them on the cooking sheet and baking them.

Notes

Drinks

Almond Fruit Tea Spritzer

This is a twist on our almond fruit tea. It makes a nice punch for bridal and baby showers. We served it on Mother's Day at the tea room. Everyone loved it and wanted the recipe. It does have a lot of sugar, so feel free to cut down on the sugar amount if you wish.

- 3 T. loose Assam tea (Leopard's Blend is great!)
- 4 cups of boiling water, plus enough cold water to fill a one gallon container
- 1 c. sugar (start with ½ c. cup and add the rest to taste, this is a very sweet tea)
- 1 6 oz. can frozen lemonade concentrate
- 2 t. almond extract
- 2 qt. chilled ginger ale

Place loose tea in a tea sock or tea infuser. Pour boiling water over the tea leaves. Steep for 4 minutes. Remove leaves from tea. In a one gallon container mix sugar, lemonade and almond extract. Add hot tea. Stir until sugar is dissolved. Fill the container with cold water and/or ice until it reaches half full (2 qt.) Chill. Immediately before serving, add the ginger ale.

Serve immediately.

This tea is also good by itself without the ginger ale.

Makes about 1 gallon.

Notes

Homemade Amaretto

My mom began making this when I was in college. She gave it out as gifts in pretty bottles tied with ribbon for the holidays. It's delicious!

- 1 lemon
- 3 c. sugar
- 2 c. water
- 3 c. vodka
- 3 T. brandy
- 2 T. almond extract
- 2 t. pure vanilla extract
- 1 t. pure chocolate extract

Peel lemon, leaving inner white skin on fruit. Cut rind into 2"x¼" strips. Reserve pulp for other uses. Combine lemon peel, sugar and water in a saucepan. Bring to a boil; cover, reduce heat and simmer 30 minutes. Remove from heat. Remove lemon peel and discard. Refrigerate mixture. Stir in vodka and remaining ingredients. Store in an airtight container or bottles. This does not need to be refrigerated.

Notes

Wassail

My mom found this recipe and served it for military parties when we were growing up. I just make it on the stove and use a tea sock for the spices, but if you have a coffee urn with a percolator that's the best.

- 2 qt. apple juice
- 1½ qt. cranberry juice
- ½ c. brown sugar
- ½ t. salt
- 4 cinnamon sticks
- 1½ t. whole cloves
- 1 t. ground allspice
- ½ t. ground nutmeg

Combine all ingredients and simmer on stove for about 10-15 minutes. Strain and serve. Or use a tea sock for spices and remove before serving.

Notes

Index

Index Continued

Index Continued

About the Author

Amy Lawrence is an example for women who have had many successful careers in life, including teacher and business owner. With a master's degree in Special Education, she taught for 11 years. In 2003 she decided to pursue her passion and opened her tea room, An Afternoon to Remember. It won many awards including Best Small Tea Room in the U.S. in 2006, KCRA's A-List in 2007, 2008 and 2009, and Sacramento Magazine's Best Tea Room in 2008. In 2009, Amy closed her tea room in order to devote herself full-time to her family and other companies: Afternoon to Remember Fine Tea and Gifts, ATR Publishing, and the International Tea Sippers Society. Amy has published eight cookbooks and sold more than 10,000 of them. She is currently working on several new projects, including resources for new tea room owners.

Also from ATR Publishing

Creating an Afternoon to
Remember

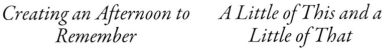

A Little of This and a
Little of That

Making It Your Own
Afternoon to Remember

Tea Time Tidbits and
Treats

Drop by for Tea

Master Tea Room
Recipes

*Order them online at
http://www.afternoontoremember.com/*

Breinigsville, PA USA
19 April 2010
236448BV00001B/40/P